The Senior Goldendoodle 's Guide To Preventive Veterinary Medicine

Roberto Miguel Rodriguez and Bradley James Loch

Copyright Page

TITLE: The Senior Goldendoodle's Guide to Preventive Veterinary Medicine

1ST Edition

Copyright @ 2023

ISBN: 9798223768821

Table of Contents

The Senior Goldendoodle's Guide to Preventive Veterinary Medicine

By Roberto Miguel Rodriguez and Bradley James Loch

Chapter 1: Introduction to Preventive Veterinary Medicine for a Senior Goldendoodle Dog

Understanding the Importance of Preventive Veterinary Medicine

As a loving pet owner, you want to ensure the well-being and longevity of your senior Goldendoodle. One of the most effective ways to achieve this is through preventive veterinary medicine. By taking a proactive approach to your dog's healthcare, you can help prevent the onset of diseases, detect potential health issues early, and provide your furry friend with a higher quality of life.

Preventive veterinary medicine encompasses a wide range of areas that are crucial for the overall health and wellness of your senior Goldendoodle. From preventive dental care to reproductive health, each aspect plays a vital role in ensuring your dog remains happy and healthy in their golden years.

Regular dental care is essential for your senior Goldendoodle's oral health. Dental problems, such as gum disease and tooth decay, can lead to pain, infection, and even heart disease. By implementing preventive dental care practices, such as regular teeth brushing and professional cleanings, you can keep your dog's teeth and gums in optimal condition.

Proper nutrition and diet are also key components of preventive veterinary medicine. A balanced and age-appropriate diet can help prevent obesity, maintain a healthy weight, and provide the necessary nutrients for your senior Goldendoodle's overall well-being.

Maintaining your dog's joint and mobility health is crucial as they age. Regular exercise, joint supplements, and appropriate pain management can help prevent the onset of arthritis and other joint-related conditions, ensuring your senior Goldendoodle remains active and pain-free.

Just like humans, dogs can experience vision problems as they age. Regular eye exams and preventive care can help detect and address any issues promptly, preventing further deterioration of their vision.

A healthy skin and coat are not only aesthetically pleasing but also indicative of your dog's overall health. Preventive care, such as regular grooming, flea and tick control, and skin checks, can help identify and treat any skin conditions early on.

Heart and cardiovascular health is another crucial aspect of preventive veterinary medicine. Regular check-ups, heartworm prevention, and a heart-healthy diet can help prevent heart disease and ensure your senior Goldendoodle's cardiovascular system remains in good shape.

Cognitive and brain health are important for your dog's mental well-being. Engaging in mentally stimulating activities, providing a balanced diet rich in brain-boosting nutrients, and regular veterinary check-ups can help maintain optimal cognitive function as your senior Goldendoodle ages.

Parasite control is essential to prevent the transmission of diseases and keep your dog healthy. Regular vaccinations, flea and tick prevention, and deworming protocols can help protect your senior Goldendoodle from harmful parasites.

Reproductive health care is important, even for senior dogs. Spaying or neutering your Goldendoodle can help prevent certain diseases and behavioral issues, ensuring a healthier and happier life for your furry companion.

Lastly, preventive emotional and behavioral care is crucial for the well-being of your senior Goldendoodle. Regular exercise, mental stimulation, and addressing any behavioral concerns can help prevent anxiety, depression, and other emotional issues that may arise as your dog ages.

By understanding and implementing the importance of preventive veterinary medicine, you can provide your senior Goldendoodle with the best possible care. Regular veterinary check-ups, proper nutrition, dental care, exercise, and preventive measures will ensure your furry friend remains healthy, happy, and by your side for many more years to come.

The Benefits of Early Intervention and Regular Check-ups

When it comes to the health and well-being of your senior Goldendoodle, early intervention and regular check-ups are essential. By taking a proactive approach to preventive veterinary medicine, you can ensure that your furry friend enjoys a longer, healthier, and more fulfilling life.

Early intervention is crucial because it allows for the detection and treatment of potential health issues before they become serious. Regular check-ups provide an opportunity for your veterinarian to assess your dog's overall health and address any concerns that may arise. By catching problems early on, you can prevent them from worsening and potentially causing more harm to your furry companion.

One of the key benefits of early intervention is the ability to identify and manage common age-related conditions. From joint and mobility issues to dental problems, senior Goldendoodles are prone to various health concerns. By detecting these issues early, you can take proactive measures to manage them, such as implementing a preventive joint care regimen or scheduling regular dental cleanings.

Regular check-ups also play a vital role in preventive nutrition and diet for senior Goldendoodles. As dogs age, their nutritional needs change, and it's important to ensure they are receiving the right balance of nutrients. During check-ups, your veterinarian can assess your dog's dietary needs and make recommendations for a senior-specific diet that promotes optimal health and vitality.

Additionally, preventive check-ups are essential for maintaining your senior Goldendoodle's cognitive and brain health. Cognitive decline is a common concern in aging dogs, but early intervention can help slow its progression. Your veterinarian can provide guidance on brain-stimulating activities, supplements, and medications that may benefit your furry friend.

Furthermore, regular check-ups allow for preventive parasite control, which is crucial for senior Goldendoodles. As dogs age, their immune systems may weaken, making them more susceptible to parasites such as fleas, ticks, and worms. By implementing a preventive parasite control program, you can protect your dog from these harmful pests and the diseases they carry.

Lastly, regular check-ups provide an opportunity to address your senior Goldendoodle's emotional and behavioral needs. Aging can bring about changes in behavior, such as increased anxiety or aggression. By discussing these concerns with your veterinarian, you can develop a plan to support your dog's emotional well-being and address any behavioral issues that may arise.

In conclusion, early intervention and regular check-ups are essential for the preventive veterinary care of your senior Goldendoodle. By taking a proactive approach to your dog's health, you can detect and manage potential issues before they become serious, ensuring that your furry friend enjoys a long and healthy life.

How this Guide Can Help You Care for Your Senior Goldendoodle

Welcome to "The Senior Goldendoodle's Guide to Preventive Veterinary Medicine." This comprehensive guide is designed to assist you in providing the best possible care for your beloved senior Goldendoodle. By following the preventive measures outlined in this book, you can ensure that your furry companion leads a healthy, happy, and fulfilling life.

Preventive veterinary medicine is crucial for senior Goldendoodles. As your dog ages, certain health issues become more prevalent, and it is essential to address them proactively. This guide covers a wide range of topics, including dental care, nutrition, joint and mobility care, eye and vision care, skin and coat care, heart and cardiovascular care, cognitive and brain health care, parasite control, reproductive health care, and emotional and behavioral care.

One of the key aspects discussed in this guide is preventive dental care. Dental problems, such as gum disease and tooth decay, can lead to more severe health issues if left untreated. We provide you with tips on how to maintain your senior Goldendoodle's oral health and prevent dental problems.

Another crucial topic covered is preventive nutrition and diet. As your Goldendoodle ages, their nutritional needs change. Our guide offers advice on choosing the right diet, portion control, and supplements to support your dog's overall health and well-being.

Joint and mobility care is also a significant concern for senior Goldendoodles. We discuss the importance of exercise, weight management, and joint supplements to keep your dog active and pain-free.

Additionally, this guide addresses preventive eye and vision care, skin and coat care, heart and cardiovascular care, cognitive and brain health care, parasite control, reproductive health care, and emotional and behavioral care. Each chapter provides practical tips and recommendations to help you create a preventive care routine tailored to your senior Goldendoodle's needs.

By incorporating the preventive measures outlined in this guide into your senior Goldendoodle's lifestyle, you can significantly enhance their quality of life and minimize the risk of developing age-related health issues. Remember, prevention is always better than cure, and with this guide by your side, you can become your dog's trusted health advocate.

Whether you are new to owning a senior Goldendoodle or have had one for years, this guide is a valuable resource for every dog owner. We encourage you to read it thoroughly, consult with your veterinarian, and take proactive steps to ensure your senior Goldendoodle's well-being. Together, we can provide the best possible care for our furry companions and cherish the wonderful moments we share with them.

Chapter 2: Preventive Dental Care for Senior Goldendoodle Dogs

Dental Health Issues Common in Senior Goldendoodles

As our beloved Goldendoodles enter their senior years, it is crucial to pay close attention to their dental health. Just like humans, dogs can experience a range of dental issues that can lead to discomfort, pain, and even more severe health problems if left untreated. In this subchapter, we will explore some of the most common dental health issues that senior Goldendoodles may face and discuss preventive measures to keep their teeth and gums healthy.

One of the most prevalent dental problems in senior Goldendoodles is periodontal disease. This condition occurs when plaque and tartar build-up on the teeth, leading to inflammation of the gums and potential damage to the tooth roots. As the disease progresses, it can cause tooth loss and even affect vital organs, such as the heart and kidneys. Regular dental cleanings and daily toothbrushing can help prevent periodontal disease and maintain good oral hygiene.

Another dental issue that senior Goldendoodles may encounter is tooth decay. This can occur due to a combination of factors, including poor dental hygiene, a sugary diet, and genetic predisposition. Regular dental check-ups, along with a balanced and nutritious diet, can help minimize the risk of tooth decay. Additionally, avoiding feeding your Goldendoodle foods that are high in sugar or harmful to their teeth, such as hard bones or chew toys, can further protect their dental health.

Furthermore, senior Goldendoodles may be prone to developing oral tumors, cysts, or other abnormal growths in their mouths. These growths can cause discomfort or difficulty eating and may require surgical intervention. Regular dental examinations by a veterinarian can help detect any abnormalities early on, allowing for prompt treatment and a better prognosis.

In conclusion, senior Goldendoodles are susceptible to various dental health issues that can significantly impact their overall well-being. By implementing preventive measures such as regular dental cleanings, daily toothbrushing, a balanced diet, and routine check-ups, we can minimize the risk of these problems and ensure our furry friends enjoy a happy and healthy life in their golden years. Remember, a healthy smile equals a happy Goldendoodle!

Brushing Your Senior Goldendoodle's Teeth

Maintaining your senior Goldendoodle's oral health is crucial to their overall well-being. Regular dental care can prevent a range of dental issues, including gum disease, tooth decay, and bad breath. In this subchapter, we will discuss the importance of brushing your senior Goldendoodle's teeth and provide you with some tips on how to make the process easier.

As your Goldendoodle ages, their teeth become more susceptible to dental problems. Plaque and tartar can build up on their teeth, leading to gum disease and other oral health issues. By brushing your dog's teeth regularly, you can remove this buildup and prevent dental problems from occurring.

To start, you will need a toothbrush and toothpaste specifically designed for dogs. Human toothpaste contains ingredients that can be harmful to dogs, so it's important to choose a toothpaste that is safe for them. You can find dog-friendly toothbrushes and toothpaste at your local pet store or ask your veterinarian for recommendations.

Begin by introducing your senior Goldendoodle to the toothbrush and toothpaste gradually. Let them sniff and lick the toothpaste to get used to the taste. Once they are comfortable, gently lift their lips and brush their teeth using circular motions. Focus on the outside surfaces of their teeth, as this is where plaque tends to accumulate. Be sure to reach the back teeth as well.

If your senior Goldendoodle is resistant to having their teeth brushed, you can try using a finger brush or a piece of gauze wrapped around your finger. This can be less intimidating for them and still effectively clean their teeth.

Ideally, you should aim to brush your dog's teeth at least three times a week. However, even brushing once a week can make a significant difference in their oral health. Additionally, providing dental chews or toys can help remove plaque and tartar between brushing sessions.

In conclusion, regular brushing is essential for maintaining your senior Goldendoodle's dental health. By incorporating this simple task into your pet's routine, you can prevent dental problems and ensure their overall well-being. Remember to use dog-friendly toothbrushes and toothpaste, introduce the process gradually, and make it a positive experience for your furry friend. Your senior Goldendoodle will thank you with a healthy and happy smile!

Professional Dental Cleanings and Other Dental Procedures

Maintaining good oral hygiene is essential for the overall health and well-being of your senior Goldendoodle. Dental problems can lead to pain, infection, and even systemic health issues if left untreated. In this subchapter, we will discuss the importance of professional dental cleanings and other dental procedures for your furry friend.

Professional dental cleanings are a crucial part of preventive veterinary medicine for senior Goldendoodle dogs. While regular brushing at home is important, it is not enough to remove all the plaque and tartar buildup that can accumulate on your dog's teeth and gums. During a professional dental cleaning, a veterinarian will use specialized tools to remove the plaque and tartar from your dog's teeth, both above and below the gumline. This process, known as scaling, helps prevent the development of periodontal disease, which can lead to tooth loss and other serious health problems.

In addition to dental cleanings, there are other dental procedures that may be necessary for your senior Goldendoodle. These include dental X-rays, tooth extractions, and treatment for dental diseases such as gingivitis or abscesses. Dental X-rays can reveal hidden problems beneath the gumline, such as tooth root infections or fractured teeth. Tooth extractions may be necessary if a tooth is severely decayed or damaged beyond repair. Treating dental diseases promptly is essential to prevent further complications and ensure your dog's comfort and well-being.

Preventive dental care for senior Goldendoodle dogs also includes regular dental check-ups and at-home dental care. During check-ups, a veterinarian will examine your dog's teeth, gums, and mouth for any signs of dental issues. They can also provide guidance on proper brushing techniques and recommend dental products that are safe and effective for your furry friend.

Remember, preventive veterinary medicine is essential for maintaining your senior Goldendoodle's overall health and quality of life. By prioritizing your dog's dental health and seeking professional dental care when needed, you can help ensure that they enjoy a healthy and happy life for years to come.

Chapter 3: Preventive Nutrition and Diet for Senior Goldendoodle Dogs

Nutritional Requirements for Senior Goldendoodles

As our beloved Goldendoodles enter their golden years, it becomes essential for us, as responsible pet owners, to pay extra attention to their nutritional needs. A well-balanced diet plays a crucial role in maintaining their overall health and preventing various age-related issues. In this subchapter, we will explore the nutritional requirements specifically tailored for senior Goldendoodles.

As senior Goldendoodles tend to have lower energy levels and a slower metabolism, it is important to adjust their calorie intake accordingly. A diet rich in lean protein, such as chicken or fish, is vital for maintaining muscle mass and supporting organ function. However, portion control becomes essential to prevent obesity, which can lead to joint problems and other health issues.

Senior Goldendoodles also benefit from a diet that includes high-quality carbohydrates, such as whole grains and vegetables. These provide them with energy and essential nutrients like fiber, vitamins, and minerals. Additionally, including healthy fats, like omega-3 fatty acids found in fish oil, can help support their cognitive function and maintain a healthy coat and skin.

It is crucial to monitor your senior Goldendoodle's weight and body condition regularly. Consulting with a veterinarian can help determine the ideal weight and recommend appropriate portion sizes. Moreover, consider incorporating supplements into their diet to support their joint health, such as glucosamine and chondroitin.

As dental health tends to deteriorate with age, it is important to choose a diet that promotes good oral hygiene. Opting for dry kibble, dental chews, or incorporating regular teeth brushing into their routine can help prevent dental issues like gum disease and tooth decay.

Always provide fresh and clean water for your senior Goldendoodle to prevent dehydration, especially if they suffer from any kidney or urinary issues.

Remember, each dog is unique, and their nutritional needs may vary. Regular check-ups with a veterinarian can help ensure that your senior Goldendoodle's dietary requirements are met and any specific health concerns are addressed.

By providing a well-balanced and tailored diet, we can support our senior Goldendoodles' overall well-being and help them age gracefully, maintaining their vitality and enjoying their golden years to the fullest.

Choosing the Right Senior Goldendoodle Food

As your beloved Goldendoodle enters their senior years, it is important to make adjustments to their diet to ensure they continue to live a healthy and fulfilling life. Choosing the right senior Goldendoodle food is crucial for their overall well-being, as it can help prevent various health issues and support their specific needs.

Senior Goldendoodles have different dietary requirements compared to younger dogs. They may have slower metabolisms, decreased appetite, and specific health concerns that need to be addressed through their diet. When selecting a senior Goldendoodle food, there are several factors to consider.

First and foremost, it is essential to look for a high-quality dog food that is specifically formulated for senior dogs. These foods are typically lower in calories to prevent weight gain, which can put additional strain on their joints and organs. They also contain higher levels of nutrients such as antioxidants, vitamins, and minerals to support their immune system and overall health.

Another crucial consideration is the protein content of the food. Senior Goldendoodles may require higher levels of protein to maintain their muscle mass and support their aging bodies. Look for a food that lists a high-quality source of protein, such as chicken or fish, as the first ingredient.

Additionally, it is important to choose a senior Goldendoodle food that contains healthy fats, such as omega-3 fatty acids. These fats can help support their joint health, cognitive function, and promote a healthy coat and skin. Look for ingredients like fish oil or flaxseed oil in the food's ingredient list.

When transitioning your senior Goldendoodle to a new food, it is important to do so gradually. Make sure to mix the new food with their current food over a period of several days to avoid any digestive upset. Monitor their eating habits and consult with your veterinarian if you have any concerns or questions.

In conclusion, choosing the right senior Goldendoodle food is essential for their overall health and well-being. Consider their specific needs, such as slower metabolism and potential health issues, and look for a high-quality food that addresses these concerns. By providing them with the proper nutrition, you can help ensure that your senior Goldendoodle enjoys their golden years to the fullest.

Supplements and Special Dietary Considerations for Senior Goldendoodles

As your beloved Goldendoodle enters their golden years, it becomes increasingly important to provide them with the necessary supplements and special dietary considerations to ensure their health and well-being. In this subchapter, we will explore the various supplements and dietary adjustments that can benefit senior Goldendoodles, helping them age gracefully and maintain optimal health.

One of the key considerations for senior Goldendoodles is joint and mobility care. As they age, their joints can become stiff and arthritic, leading to discomfort and decreased mobility. Omega-3 fatty acids, such as fish oil, can help reduce inflammation and promote joint health. Glucosamine and chondroitin supplements are also beneficial in supporting joint function and reducing the development of arthritis.

In addition to joint health, cognitive and brain health care is crucial for senior Goldendoodles. Antioxidants, vitamins C and E, and omega-3 fatty acids can help protect brain cells from oxidative stress and promote cognitive function. These nutrients can be obtained through a balanced diet or supplemented if necessary.

Heart and cardiovascular care is another important aspect of preventive veterinary medicine for senior Goldendoodles. Coenzyme Q10 and omega-3 fatty acids can support heart health and reduce the risk of cardiovascular diseases. It is essential to consult with your veterinarian to determine the appropriate dosage for your dog.

Ensuring proper nutrition and diet for senior Goldendoodles is vital in maintaining their overall health. As they age, their metabolism slows down, and they may require fewer calories. High-quality senior dog food formulated specifically for their needs can provide the necessary nutrients while managing their weight. Additionally, incorporating fresh fruits and vegetables into their diet can boost their immune system and provide essential vitamins and minerals.

It is worth noting that while supplements can be beneficial, they should not replace a balanced diet. Always consult with your veterinarian before introducing any new supplements to your senior Goldendoodle's routine.

By addressing their specific needs through supplements and special dietary considerations, you can help your senior Goldendoodle age gracefully and enjoy their golden years to the fullest. Remember, preventive veterinary medicine plays a crucial role in maintaining their overall health, and regular check-ups with your veterinarian are essential to address any potential issues proactively.

Chapter 4: Preventive Joint and Mobility Care for Senior Goldendoodle Dogs

Common Joint and Mobility Issues in Senior Goldendoodles

As our adorable Goldendoodles age, it is important to be aware of the common joint and mobility issues that they may face. Just like humans, senior dogs can experience a decline in mobility and develop joint problems that can significantly impact their quality of life. In this subchapter, we will discuss the common joint and mobility issues that senior Goldendoodles may encounter and how to prevent and manage them.

One of the most prevalent joint issues in senior Goldendoodles is osteoarthritis. This degenerative condition affects the joints, causing pain, stiffness, and difficulty in movement. Regular exercise, maintaining a healthy weight, and providing joint supplements can help prevent and manage osteoarthritis in senior Goldendoodles.

Another common joint problem is hip dysplasia, which is a genetic condition that causes the hip joints to develop abnormally. This can lead to pain, lameness, and difficulty in getting up or walking. Regular veterinary check-ups, proper nutrition, and avoiding excessive jumping or rough play can help reduce the risk of hip dysplasia in senior Goldendoodles.

Senior Goldendoodles may also develop intervertebral disc disease, a condition that affects the spinal discs and can cause pain, weakness, and paralysis. Preventive measures such as avoiding excessive jumping, providing proper support during lifting, and regular exercise can help reduce the risk of intervertebral disc disease.

It is essential to be vigilant for signs of joint and mobility issues in our senior Goldendoodles. These may include difficulty in getting up or lying down, reluctance to jump or climb stairs, limping, and decreased activity levels. If you notice any of these signs, it is crucial to consult with your veterinarian for a proper diagnosis and treatment plan.

In conclusion, joint and mobility issues are common in senior Goldendoodles, but there are preventive measures that can be taken to reduce the risk and manage these conditions. Regular veterinary check-ups, proper nutrition, weight management, exercise, and supplements can all contribute to maintaining the joint health and mobility of our beloved senior Goldendoodles. By being proactive and attentive to their needs, we can help ensure that they enjoy a happy and active life in their golden years.

Exercise and Physical Activity for Senior Goldendoodles

As your beloved Goldendoodle enters their golden years, it becomes even more important to prioritize their overall health and well-being. One crucial aspect of preventive veterinary medicine for senior Goldendoodles is exercise and physical activity. Regular exercise not only helps maintain a healthy weight but also promotes cardiovascular fitness, joint mobility, cognitive function, and emotional well-being.

When it comes to exercise for senior Goldendoodles, it's essential to strike a balance between keeping them active and preventing any potential injuries or strain. Here are some guidelines and tips to help you provide the right amount of exercise for your senior Goldendoodle:

1. Consult with your veterinarian: Before starting any exercise regimen, consult with your veterinarian to ensure your senior Goldendoodle is in good health and can handle physical activity. They can provide specific recommendations based on your dog's individual needs and any underlying health conditions.

2. Low-impact activities: Opt for low-impact activities that are gentle on your senior Goldendoodle's joints. Walking is an excellent exercise choice, and you can gradually increase the duration and intensity as your dog tolerates. Swimming is another fantastic option as it provides a full-body workout without putting stress on the joints.

3. Mental stimulation: Incorporate mental stimulation into your senior Goldendoodle's exercise routine. Puzzle toys, obedience training, and interactive games can help keep their mind sharp and prevent cognitive decline.

4. Playdates and socialization: Engaging in playdates or supervised interactions with other dogs can provide socialization opportunities for your senior Goldendoodle. This can help prevent behavioral issues and keep them mentally and emotionally stimulated.

5. Regular check-ins: Pay attention to your senior Goldendoodle's energy levels and overall well-being. If they seem fatigued or show signs of discomfort during or after exercise, it may be necessary to adjust their routine or consult with your veterinarian.

Remember, every senior Goldendoodle is unique, and their exercise needs may vary. Some dogs may require more frequent, shorter sessions, while others may still have the stamina for longer walks. Be attentive to your dog's individual needs and adjust their exercise routine accordingly.

In conclusion, regular exercise and physical activity are vital components of preventive veterinary medicine for senior Goldendoodles. By providing appropriate exercise, you can help maintain their overall health, joint mobility, cognitive function, and emotional well-being. Always consult with your veterinarian to ensure you are providing the right amount and type of exercise for your senior Goldendoodle's specific needs.

Joint Supplements and Therapies for Senior Goldendoodles

As our beloved Goldendoodles age, it's important to provide them with the necessary care and support to maintain their joint health and mobility. Joint problems are common in senior dogs, but with the right preventive measures, we can help them live a comfortable and active life. In this subchapter, we will explore the various joint supplements and therapies available for senior Goldendoodles.

One of the key supplements recommended for joint health is glucosamine. Glucosamine is a natural compound that helps maintain the integrity of cartilage and reduce inflammation in the joints. It can be found in many pet stores and is available in different forms such as chewable tablets or liquid supplements. Adding glucosamine to your senior Goldendoodle's daily routine can provide them with the support they need to keep their joints strong and flexible.

Another popular supplement is omega-3 fatty acids, which have been shown to have anti-inflammatory properties and promote joint health. You can find omega-3 fatty acids in fish oil supplements, which can be added to your dog's food. These supplements not only benefit their joint health but also contribute to their overall well-being.

In addition to supplements, certain therapies can also help alleviate joint pain and improve mobility in senior Goldendoodles. Physical therapy, including exercises and stretches, can help strengthen the muscles around the joints and improve range of motion. Hydrotherapy, which involves exercises in water, is particularly beneficial for dogs with joint problems as it reduces stress on their joints while still providing a great workout.

Acupuncture is another alternative therapy that has shown promising results in relieving joint pain and improving mobility. By stimulating specific points on your Goldendoodle's body, acupuncture can help release natural pain-relieving chemicals and promote healing.

Remember, it's important to consult with your veterinarian before starting any supplements or therapies. They will be able to recommend the most suitable options for your senior Goldendoodle based on their individual needs and condition.

By providing the right joint supplements and therapies, we can ensure that our senior Goldendoodles continue to enjoy an active and pain-free life well into their golden years.

Chapter 5: Preventive Eye and Vision Care for Senior Goldendoodle Dogs

Common Eye and Vision Problems in Senior Goldendoodles

As our beloved Goldendoodles age, it is important to pay close attention to their eye health and vision. Just like humans, senior dogs can develop a range of eye problems that may affect their quality of life. In this subchapter, we will explore some common eye and vision problems that senior Goldendoodles may face and discuss preventive measures to keep their eyes healthy.

One common issue in senior Goldendoodles is cataracts. Cataracts occur when the lens of the eye becomes cloudy, leading to blurred vision or even blindness. Regular eye examinations by a veterinarian can help detect cataracts early on, and in some cases, surgical intervention may be necessary to remove them. However, there are preventive measures that can delay the onset of cataracts, such as a balanced diet rich in antioxidants, regular exercise, and protecting the eyes from excessive sun exposure.

Another eye problem that senior Goldendoodles may experience is dry eye, also known as keratoconjunctivitis sicca. This condition occurs when the eyes do not produce enough tears, resulting in discomfort, redness, and potential damage to the cornea. Preventive care for dry eye includes maintaining proper hydration, using prescribed eye drops or ointments, and avoiding exposure to irritants such as smoke or dust.

Glaucoma is another eye condition that can affect senior Goldendoodles. It is characterized by increased pressure within the eye, which can lead to vision loss if left untreated. Regular eye pressure monitoring and early detection are crucial for managing glaucoma. Treatment options may include medication, surgery, or a combination of both.

Additionally, senior Goldendoodles may be prone to age-related macular degeneration, a condition that affects the central part of the retina and can cause vision loss. While there is no cure for macular degeneration, a nutritious diet rich in vitamins C and E, beta-carotene, zinc, and omega-3 fatty acids can help slow its progression.

In conclusion, as our Goldendoodles age, it is important to prioritize their eye health and vision. Regular veterinary check-ups, a balanced diet, and preventive measures can go a long way in maintaining their eye health and preventing common eye problems. By being proactive and attentive to their needs, we can ensure that our senior Goldendoodles enjoy a happy and healthy life.

Regular Eye Exams and Monitoring for Senior Goldendoodles

As our beloved Goldendoodles enter their senior years, it becomes increasingly important to prioritize their overall health and well-being. One area that requires special attention is their eye health. Just like humans, senior dogs may experience age-related changes and develop various eye conditions. To ensure their eyes remain healthy and their vision remains sharp, regular eye exams and monitoring are crucial.

Regular eye exams allow veterinarians to detect any potential issues early on, preventing them from progressing into more serious conditions. During these exams, your veterinarian will thoroughly examine your senior Goldendoodle's eyes, checking for any signs of redness, inflammation, or discharge. They will also assess the clarity of their vision and evaluate the health of the structures within the eye, including the cornea, lens, and retina.

Senior Goldendoodles are prone to several eye conditions, including cataracts, glaucoma, and dry eye syndrome. Cataracts occur when the lens of the eye becomes cloudy, leading to vision impairment. Glaucoma is characterized by increased pressure within the eye, which can cause pain and irreversible damage to the optic nerve. Dry eye syndrome, on the other hand, is a condition where the eyes do not produce enough tears, leading to discomfort and potential corneal damage.

By regularly monitoring your senior Goldendoodle's eyes, you can catch these conditions early and seek appropriate treatment. Your veterinarian may recommend specialized eye drops, medications, or even surgery, depending on the specific condition. Early intervention can help preserve your dog's vision and alleviate any discomfort they may be experiencing.

In addition to regular eye exams, there are also steps you can take at home to promote good eye health for your senior Goldendoodle. Keep their eyes clean by gently wiping away any discharge or debris with a soft, damp cloth. Avoid using harsh chemicals or products near their eyes, as this can cause irritation. Additionally, make sure their environment is free from potential hazards that could cause eye injuries.

Remember, preventive care is key to maintaining your senior Goldendoodle's overall health and quality of life. By prioritizing regular eye exams and monitoring, you can help ensure that their eyes remain healthy and their vision remains clear well into their golden years.

Caring for Your Senior Goldendoodle's Eyes at Home

As your beloved Goldendoodle ages, it becomes increasingly important to provide them with the proper care to maintain their overall health and well-being. One area that often goes overlooked is their eye health. Just like humans, senior Goldendoodles can develop a variety of eye conditions that can affect their vision and quality of life. In this subchapter, we will discuss the importance of preventive eye and vision care for your senior Goldendoodle and provide you with some tips on how to care for their eyes at home.

Regularly examining your senior Goldendoodle's eyes is crucial in identifying any potential issues early on. Keep an eye out for symptoms such as redness, discharge, cloudiness, excessive tearing, or changes in their behavior, which may indicate discomfort or vision problems. If you notice any of these signs, it is recommended to schedule an appointment with a veterinarian who specializes in eye care for pets.

In addition to regular vet check-ups, there are steps you can take at home to promote good eye health for your senior Goldendoodle. Firstly, keep their eyes clean and free from debris by gently wiping them with a soft, damp cloth. Avoid using harsh chemicals or products not specifically formulated for pet eye care, as they can cause irritation.

Another important aspect of maintaining your senior Goldendoodle's eye health is ensuring they have a balanced diet rich in essential nutrients. Omega-3 fatty acids, antioxidants, and vitamins A, C, and E are particularly beneficial for eye health. Consult with your veterinarian to determine the appropriate diet and supplements for your dog's specific needs.

Lastly, protect your senior Goldendoodle's eyes from potential hazards, such as sharp objects, chemicals, or excessive sunlight. When outdoors, consider using doggy sunglasses or a hat with a brim to shield their eyes from harmful UV rays.

In conclusion, proactive and preventive eye care is crucial to ensuring your senior Goldendoodle's overall health and quality of life. By regularly examining their eyes, keeping them clean, providing a nutritious diet, and protecting them from potential hazards, you can help maintain their eye health as they age. Remember, early detection and intervention are key to addressing any potential eye problems, so always consult with a veterinarian if you notice any concerning symptoms.

Chapter 6: Preventive Skin and Coat Care for Senior Goldendoodle Dogs

Skin and Coat Issues Common in Senior Goldendoodles

Skin and coat issues are common in senior Goldendoodles, and it's important for pet owners to be aware of these issues to ensure the overall health and well-being of their furry companions. In this subchapter, we will discuss the most common skin and coat issues that senior Goldendoodles may face and provide preventive measures to keep their skin and coat in optimal condition.

As Goldendoodles age, their skin becomes more sensitive and prone to various issues. One common problem is dry skin, which can cause itchiness and discomfort. To prevent dry skin, it's essential to provide your senior Goldendoodle with a balanced and nutritious diet. Omega-3 fatty acids, found in fish oil supplements or certain foods like salmon, can help maintain healthy skin and coat.

Another common skin issue in senior Goldendoodles is dermatitis, which refers to inflammation of the skin. Dermatitis can be caused by various factors such as allergies, parasites, or bacterial and fungal infections. Regular grooming and bathing can help prevent dermatitis by keeping your dog's skin clean and free from allergens or irritants. It's also important to use gentle, hypoallergenic shampoos and conditioners specifically designed for dogs.

Senior Goldendoodles are also prone to developing skin tumors, such as lipomas or sebaceous adenomas. Regularly checking your dog's skin for any lumps or bumps and consulting with a veterinarian is crucial for early detection and proper treatment.

Additionally, senior Goldendoodles may experience coat changes, such as thinning or dullness. These changes can be attributed to aging and hormonal imbalances. Regular grooming, including brushing and regular haircuts, can help maintain a healthy coat and prevent matting.

In conclusion, skin and coat issues are common in senior Goldendoodles, but with proper preventive care, these issues can be minimized or even avoided. By providing a nutritious diet, regular grooming, and monitoring your dog's skin and coat, you can ensure that your senior Goldendoodle maintains healthy skin and a lustrous coat throughout their golden years. Remember, early detection and intervention are key to preventing more severe skin and coat issues, so it's important to consult with a veterinarian if you notice any abnormalities.

Grooming and Bathing Your Senior Goldendoodle

As your beloved Goldendoodle enters their senior years, it becomes even more important to prioritize their grooming and bathing routine. Regular grooming and bathing not only keep your furry friend looking and smelling fresh, but it also plays a crucial role in their overall health and well-being. In this subchapter, we will explore the essential aspects of grooming and bathing for senior Goldendoodles.

Grooming your senior Goldendoodle should include brushing their coat regularly to prevent matting and tangling. As your dog ages, their coat may become thinner, so using a soft-bristle brush or a comb designed for senior dogs is recommended. Regular brushing helps distribute natural oils, stimulates the skin, and promotes healthy hair growth.

Additionally, it allows you to check for any skin abnormalities, such as lumps, bumps, or rashes, that may require veterinary attention.

Bathing your senior Goldendoodle should be done when necessary, taking into consideration their individual needs and activity level. Older dogs may have sensitive skin, so it is crucial to use a mild, hypoallergenic shampoo specifically formulated for senior dogs. Remember to thoroughly rinse off all the shampoo and ensure your dog is completely dry before allowing them to go outside, as they may be more susceptible to temperature changes.

While grooming and bathing are important, it is equally crucial to pay attention to other areas of your senior Goldendoodle's preventive care. Regular dental cleanings and check-ups are vital to maintain their oral health and prevent periodontal disease. Senior dogs may also benefit from a specialized diet that supports their changing nutritional needs, as well as joint supplements to promote mobility and reduce the risk of arthritis.

Furthermore, regular eye examinations can help detect and address any vision problems that may arise with age. Skincare should not be overlooked either, as senior dogs may develop dry, itchy skin. Using moisturizing products and providing a balanced diet can help maintain a healthy skin and coat.

In addition to physical care, it is important to address your senior Goldendoodle's emotional and behavioral well-being. Engaging them in mental stimulation activities and providing a calm and supportive environment can help prevent cognitive decline and promote a positive state of mind.

Lastly, parasite control and reproductive health should also be considered. Regular check-ups with a veterinarian will ensure your dog is protected against fleas, ticks, and other parasites. If you have not already done so, spaying or neutering your senior Goldendoodle can prevent certain reproductive health issues and contribute to their overall well-being.

By prioritizing grooming and bathing, along with comprehensive preventive care, you can ensure that your senior Goldendoodle enjoys a happy, healthy, and comfortable life in their golden years.

Skin and Coat Supplements and Care Products for Senior Goldendoodles

As your beloved Goldendoodle enters their senior years, it is important to provide them with the proper care to ensure they stay healthy and comfortable. One aspect of their well-being that requires attention is their skin and coat. Aging can bring about changes in your dog's skin and coat, such as dryness, thinning, and dullness. Fortunately, there are various skin and coat supplements and care products available that can help maintain their skin's health and keep their coat looking lustrous.

One essential supplement for senior Goldendoodles is omega-3 fatty acids. These healthy fats not only promote a healthy skin and coat but also have numerous other benefits, such as reducing inflammation and supporting cognitive function. Omega-3 fatty acids can be found in fish oil supplements specifically formulated for dogs. Adding this supplement to your senior Goldendoodle's diet can help alleviate dry skin and promote a soft, shiny coat.

In addition to omega-3 fatty acids, there are also specific supplements available that target skin and coat health. These supplements often contain ingredients like biotin, zinc, and vitamins A and E, which are known to support skin and coat health. These supplements come in the form of tasty chewable tablets or powders that can be easily mixed into your dog's food.

Aside from supplements, there are also a variety of care products that can help maintain your senior Goldendoodle's skin and coat. Regular brushing is essential to remove loose hair, prevent matting, and stimulate the production of natural oils that keep the coat healthy. Look for brushes specifically designed for Goldendoodles, as their unique coat requires special attention.

When bathing your senior Goldendoodle, choose a gentle shampoo that is formulated for sensitive skin. Avoid using human shampoos, as they can strip the natural oils from your dog's skin, leading to dryness and irritation. After bathing, consider using a moisturizing conditioner to further nourish their skin and coat.

Remember to consult with your veterinarian before introducing any new supplements or care products to your senior Goldendoodle's routine. They can provide guidance on the best products for your dog's specific needs and help ensure their overall health and well-being.

By incorporating skin and coat supplements and care products into your senior Goldendoodle's preventive veterinary medicine regimen, you can help keep them looking and feeling their best as they age gracefully.

Chapter 7: Preventive Heart and Cardiovascular Care for Senior Goldendoodle Dogs

Heart Disease and Cardiovascular Issues in Senior Goldendoodles

As our beloved Goldendoodles age, it becomes increasingly important to prioritize their overall health and well-being. One area that requires special attention is their heart and cardiovascular system. Heart disease and cardiovascular issues can affect senior Goldendoodles, just like they can in humans. By implementing preventive measures, we can help ensure a longer and healthier life for our furry companions.

Regular check-ups with a veterinarian are crucial in monitoring the cardiovascular health of senior Goldendoodles. During these visits, the vet will listen to the heart for any abnormal sounds, check the pulse, and measure blood pressure. These routine examinations can detect any early signs of heart disease or other cardiovascular issues.

Maintaining a healthy diet is also essential in preventing heart disease in senior Goldendoodles. A balanced diet that is low in sodium and rich in essential nutrients can help promote a healthy heart. Your veterinarian can provide specific dietary recommendations based on your Goldendoodle's individual needs.

Exercise plays a vital role in cardiovascular health for senior Goldendoodles. Regular physical activity helps keep the heart strong and promotes overall fitness. However, it's important to tailor exercise routines to your dog's age and physical capabilities.

Consult with your veterinarian to determine the appropriate level and type of exercise for your senior Goldendoodle.

Another preventive measure for heart health is maintaining a healthy weight. Obesity can put additional strain on the heart, leading to increased risk of heart disease. Your veterinarian can provide guidance on proper weight management strategies, including portion control and feeding guidelines.

In addition to these preventive measures, it's important to be aware of the signs and symptoms of heart disease in senior Goldendoodles. These may include coughing, difficulty breathing, lethargy, and decreased appetite. If you notice any of these symptoms or have concerns about your dog's cardiovascular health, it's important to seek veterinary care promptly.

By prioritizing preventive measures such as regular check-ups, a healthy diet, exercise, weight management, and awareness of symptoms, we can help safeguard our senior Goldendoodles against heart disease and cardiovascular issues. Remember, prevention is the key to ensuring a long and happy life for our beloved furry friends.

Regular Heart Health Check-ups for Senior Goldendoodles

As our beloved Goldendoodles enter their senior years, it becomes even more crucial to prioritize their overall health and well-being. One specific area that requires attention is their heart and cardiovascular system. Regular heart health check-ups are essential to ensure that our senior Goldendoodles maintain a strong and healthy heart.

The aging process can take a toll on our furry friends' hearts, just like it does on ours. Conditions such as heart disease, arrhythmias, and heart murmurs can develop over time. That's why preventive care and early detection are vital in maintaining their heart health.

During a regular heart health check-up, your veterinarian will perform a thorough physical examination. This includes listening to your Goldendoodle's heartbeat and checking for any irregularities or murmurs. They may also recommend additional tests such as blood work, electrocardiography (ECG), and echocardiography to evaluate the heart's structure and function.

By conducting these routine check-ups, potential heart problems can be detected early, allowing for timely intervention and treatment. This can significantly improve your senior Goldendoodle's quality of life and ensure they continue to live a happy and active lifestyle.

In addition to veterinary care, there are several steps you can take at home to promote heart health in your senior Goldendoodle. Providing a balanced and nutritious diet tailored to their specific needs is crucial. Consult with your veterinarian to determine the best diet plan for your furry friend, as certain ingredients and supplements can support heart health.

Regular exercise is also essential for maintaining cardiovascular fitness. Engaging in moderate physical activity, such as daily walks or interactive play sessions, can help keep your senior Goldendoodle's heart strong and reduce the risk of heart disease.

Lastly, keep an eye out for any changes in your Goldendoodle's behavior or overall well-being. Symptoms such as coughing, difficulty breathing, fatigue, and decreased appetite can indicate potential heart issues. If you notice any of these signs, don't hesitate to contact your veterinarian for further evaluation.

Remember, preventive care is the key to ensuring a long and healthy life for your senior Goldendoodle. By scheduling regular heart health check-ups and implementing a heart-healthy lifestyle, you can help your furry friend enjoy their golden years to the fullest.

Managing Heart Health through Diet and Exercise

Maintaining a healthy heart is crucial for the overall well-being of senior Goldendoodle dogs. Just like humans, dogs can develop heart problems as they age, making it essential for pet owners to prioritize preventive care. By incorporating the right diet and exercise routine, you can help your senior Goldendoodle live a longer, healthier life.

Diet plays a significant role in managing heart health. It is important to provide your senior Goldendoodle with a balanced and nutritious diet that promotes cardiovascular wellness. Consult with your veterinarian to determine the appropriate diet for your dog's specific needs. A heart-healthy diet typically consists of lean protein sources, such as chicken or fish, along with plenty of fruits and vegetables. Avoid foods high in sodium and unhealthy fats, as these can contribute to heart disease.

Regular exercise is equally important in maintaining heart health. Engaging in physical activity not only keeps your senior Goldendoodle's weight in check but also strengthens the heart muscle. Aim for at least 30 minutes of moderate exercise, such as brisk walks or light playtime, each day. However, be mindful of your dog's limitations and adjust the intensity of exercise according to their age and fitness level.

In addition to a healthy diet and regular exercise, there are other measures you can take to promote your senior Goldendoodle's heart health. Regular veterinary check-ups are crucial as they allow for early detection of any potential heart issues. Your veterinarian may recommend routine screenings, such as blood pressure measurements and heart function tests, to monitor your dog's cardiac health.

Supplements and medications may also be prescribed by your veterinarian to support heart health. Omega-3 fatty acids, for example, have been shown to reduce inflammation in the cardiovascular system. However, it is important to consult with your vet before adding any supplements to your senior Goldendoodle's diet.

Lastly, maintaining a stress-free environment and providing mental stimulation can contribute to your dog's overall heart health. Stress and anxiety can have negative effects on the heart, so ensure your dog feels safe and loved. Engaging in activities that challenge their brain, such as puzzle toys or obedience training, can also promote cognitive health and indirectly benefit the heart.

By managing heart health through diet, exercise, regular veterinary check-ups, and a stress-free environment, you can help your senior Goldendoodle live a long, happy, and heart-healthy life. Remember, prevention is always better than cure, and taking these preventive measures can significantly reduce the risk of heart-related problems in your beloved furry friend.

Chapter 8: Preventive Cognitive and Brain Health Care for Senior Goldendoodle Dogs

Cognitive Decline and Brain Health Issues in Senior Goldendoodles

As our beloved Goldendoodles age, it is important to understand the potential cognitive decline and brain health issues they may face. Just like humans, senior dogs can experience changes in their mental capabilities, memory, and overall brain health. In this subchapter, we will explore the preventive measures and care you can provide to ensure your senior Goldendoodle maintains optimal cognitive function.

One of the key factors in promoting brain health is mental stimulation. Engaging your senior Goldendoodle in regular mental exercises and activities can help keep their brain active and functioning at its best. This can include puzzle toys, interactive games, and training sessions that challenge their thinking and problem-solving abilities.

Another essential aspect of preventive cognitive care is a well-balanced diet. Providing your senior Goldendoodle with a nutritionally balanced diet rich in antioxidants, omega-3 fatty acids, and vitamins can support brain health. Consult your veterinarian to determine the best diet plan for your furry friend's specific needs.

Regular exercise is not only beneficial for physical health but also plays a crucial role in maintaining cognitive function. Physical activity stimulates blood flow to the brain, promoting the growth of new neurons and enhancing brain function. Take your senior Goldendoodle for daily walks, play fetch, or engage in gentle agility exercises to keep their mind and body active.

In addition to mental stimulation, diet, and exercise, it is important to schedule regular veterinary check-ups for your senior Goldendoodle. Your veterinarian can perform cognitive function tests, assess any age-related changes, and provide appropriate medical intervention if necessary. They may also recommend supplements or medications that can support brain health and slow down cognitive decline.

Lastly, maintaining a loving and stress-free environment is vital for your senior Goldendoodle's cognitive well-being. Chronic stress and anxiety can contribute to cognitive decline in dogs. Ensure your furry friend has a comfortable and safe space, provide plenty of love and attention, and minimize any sources of stress in their environment.

By implementing these preventive measures, you can help your senior Goldendoodle age gracefully and maintain optimal cognitive function. Remember, early detection and intervention are key, so always consult your veterinarian if you notice any signs of cognitive decline in your furry friend.

Mental Stimulation and Enrichment for Senior Goldendoodles

As your Goldendoodle enters their senior years, it is important to ensure that their overall health and well-being are maintained. This includes not only physical care but also mental stimulation and enrichment. Just like humans, senior dogs can experience cognitive decline and may benefit from activities that keep their minds sharp and engaged. In this subchapter, we will explore various ways to provide mental stimulation and enrichment for your senior Goldendoodle.

One of the easiest and most effective ways to stimulate your dog's mind is through interactive toys and puzzles. There are many options available on the market designed specifically for dogs, ranging from treat-dispensing toys to puzzle games. These toys encourage your Goldendoodle to use their problem-solving skills and keep them mentally engaged.

Another great way to provide mental stimulation is through training sessions. Senior dogs can still learn new tricks and commands, and training sessions provide an excellent opportunity for mental exercise. Consider teaching your Goldendoodle new commands or revisiting old ones to keep their mind sharp and their training skills intact.

Regular walks and outdoor activities are not only beneficial for physical exercise but also provide mental stimulation for your senior Goldendoodle. Exploring new environments, encountering different smells, and meeting other dogs can all contribute to keeping their minds active.

In addition to physical exercise, consider incorporating brain games and activities into your Goldendoodle's daily routine. This can include hide-and-seek games, scent training, or even basic obedience exercises. These activities not only engage their brains but also provide opportunities for bonding and interaction between you and your furry companion.

Lastly, don't forget the power of socialization. Senior dogs, just like humans, enjoy the company of others. Arrange playdates with other friendly dogs or consider enrolling your Goldendoodle in a doggy daycare program. Regular social interactions can help prevent loneliness and keep their minds stimulated.

In conclusion, mental stimulation and enrichment are essential components of preventive veterinary care for senior Goldendoodles. By incorporating interactive toys, training sessions, outdoor activities, brain games, and socialization into their daily routine, you can ensure that your furry friend remains mentally sharp, engaged, and happy in their golden years.

Supplements and Therapies for Cognitive Support in Senior Goldendoodles

As our beloved Goldendoodles age, it's important to prioritize their cognitive health and support their brain function. Just like humans, senior dogs can experience cognitive decline, which may lead to memory loss, confusion, and disorientation. However, there are various supplements and therapies available that can help maintain and improve cognitive function in senior Goldendoodles.

One supplement that has gained popularity in recent years is omega-3 fatty acids. These essential fatty acids, commonly found in fish oil, have shown promising results in supporting brain health. Omega-3s have been linked to improved memory, enhanced learning abilities, and reduced inflammation in the brain. Adding a fish oil supplement to your senior Goldendoodle's diet may help support their cognitive function.

Another supplement to consider is antioxidants. These powerful compounds help reduce oxidative stress and inflammation in the brain, both of which can contribute to cognitive decline. Antioxidants can be found in fruits and vegetables like blueberries, spinach, and broccoli. Alternatively, there are antioxidant supplements specifically formulated for dogs that can be added to their daily routine.

In addition to supplements, there are several therapies that can benefit senior Goldendoodles' cognitive health. Mental stimulation is crucial for keeping their brains active and engaged. Incorporating puzzle toys, interactive games, and training sessions into their daily routine can help maintain their cognitive function. Additionally, regular exercise is essential for overall brain health. Physical activity increases blood flow to the brain, which promotes the delivery of oxygen and nutrients necessary for optimal cognitive function.

Furthermore, senior Goldendoodles can also benefit from behavioral therapies such as reward-based training and positive reinforcement. These techniques not only enhance their cognitive abilities but also strengthen the bond between dog and owner. Engaging in activities that challenge their problem-solving skills and memory recall can be highly beneficial for their cognitive well-being.

It's important to note that before introducing any new supplement or therapy, it is recommended to consult with your veterinarian. They can provide guidance on the appropriate dosage, potential interactions, and any possible side effects. Additionally, regular check-ups with your veterinarian will ensure that your senior Goldendoodle's cognitive health is monitored and any necessary adjustments to their care plan can be made.

By incorporating supplements and therapies that support cognitive health, you can help your senior Goldendoodle maintain their mental sharpness and enjoy a fulfilling and enriched life in their golden years.

Chapter 9: Preventive Parasite Control for Senior Goldendoodle Dogs

Common Parasites That Affect Senior Goldendoodles

When it comes to the health and well-being of our beloved senior Goldendoodles, it's important to be aware of the common parasites that can affect them. These parasites can cause discomfort and health issues if left untreated, so it's crucial to take preventive measures to keep your furry friend safe and healthy.

One of the most common parasites that affect senior Goldendoodles is fleas. Fleas are tiny insects that feed on the blood of animals, causing intense itching, skin irritation, and even allergies. To prevent flea infestation, it's important to use a monthly flea preventive treatment recommended by your veterinarian. Regular grooming and vacuuming your home can also help eliminate fleas and their eggs.

Ticks are another common parasite that can affect senior Goldendoodles. These arachnids attach themselves to your dog's skin and feed on their blood. Not only can ticks cause discomfort, but they can also transmit serious diseases such as Lyme disease and Rocky Mountain spotted fever. To prevent ticks, it's important to check your dog for ticks regularly, especially after outdoor activities. Using a tick preventive treatment is also recommended, especially if you live in an area with a high tick population.

Intestinal worms, such as roundworms, hookworms, and tapeworms, are another common parasite that can affect senior

Goldendoodles. These worms can cause digestive issues, weight loss, and even anemia. To prevent intestinal worms, it's important to have your dog regularly dewormed by your veterinarian. Keeping your dog's living area clean and practicing good hygiene can also help reduce the risk of worm infestation.

Heartworms are a potentially life-threatening parasite that can affect senior Goldendoodles. These worms are transmitted through mosquito bites and can cause heart and lung damage if left untreated. To prevent heartworms, it's important to use a monthly heartworm preventive medication as recommended by your veterinarian. Regular heartworm testing is also recommended to ensure early detection and treatment if necessary.

By being aware of the common parasites that can affect senior Goldendoodles and taking preventive measures, you can help ensure the health and happiness of your furry friend. Regular veterinary check-ups and open communication with your veterinarian are key in preventing and addressing any parasite-related issues. Remember, prevention is always better than cure when it comes to protecting your senior Goldendoodle from parasites.

Year-round Parasite Prevention and Regular Testing

As a responsible pet owner, it is crucial to prioritize the preventive care of your senior Goldendoodle's health. One area that requires special attention is parasite control. Parasites can cause a range of health issues, from mild discomfort to life-threatening conditions. To ensure the well-being of your furry friend, it is important to implement year-round parasite prevention and regular testing.

Parasites can be found both internally and externally in dogs. Common internal parasites include heartworms, roundworms, hookworms, and tapeworms. These parasites can wreak havoc on your dog's digestive system, heart, and other vital organs. External parasites, such as fleas and ticks, can cause discomfort, skin allergies, and transmit diseases.

To prevent these parasites from infesting your senior Goldendoodle, you should consult with your veterinarian to establish a year-round prevention plan. This plan may include regular administration of preventive medications, such as heartworm preventives and flea and tick treatments. These medications are designed to kill and repel parasites, ensuring your dog remains protected throughout the year.

In addition to preventive medications, regular testing is essential to detect any underlying parasite infestations. Your veterinarian may recommend fecal exams to check for the presence of internal parasites. These tests can detect the presence of eggs or larvae shed by parasites in your dog's stool. By identifying and treating these infestations early on, you can prevent further complications and safeguard your dog's health.

While preventive medications and testing are vital, it is also crucial to maintain good hygiene practices. Regularly grooming your senior Goldendoodle can help identify any external parasites, such as fleas or ticks, on their fur. Additionally, keeping your dog's living environment clean and free from pests can help prevent infestations.

By prioritizing year-round parasite prevention and regular testing, you can ensure the overall health and well-being of your senior Goldendoodle. Remember to consult with your veterinarian for guidance on appropriate preventive medications and testing schedules. With proper care, you can enjoy many happy and healthy years with your beloved furry companion.

Flea, Tick, and Heartworm Prevention for Senior Goldendoodles

As our beloved Goldendoodles enter their senior years, it is essential that we continue to prioritize their preventive veterinary care. One area that requires particular attention is parasite control, including prevention of fleas, ticks, and heartworm. In this subchapter, we will discuss the importance of parasite prevention for senior Goldendoodles and provide recommendations for maintaining their health and well-being.

Fleas and ticks can cause a range of issues for our senior Goldendoodles, including skin irritation, allergic reactions, and even the transmission of diseases. To protect them from these pesky parasites, it is crucial to use a monthly flea and tick preventive medication recommended by your veterinarian. These medications come in various forms, including topical treatments and oral chewables. Your veterinarian can help you choose the most appropriate option based on your Goldendoodle's individual needs.

Heartworm disease is another potential threat to our senior Goldendoodles. Transmitted through mosquito bites, heartworms can cause severe damage to the heart and lungs, leading to life-threatening complications. To prevent this disease, your veterinarian will prescribe a monthly heartworm preventive medication. Regular testing for heartworms is also recommended, even if your Goldendoodle has been on preventive medication for years. This ensures that any potential infection is detected and treated promptly.

In addition to medication, there are other preventive measures you can take to minimize the risk of fleas, ticks, and heartworms. Regular grooming, including thorough brushing and inspection of your Goldendoodle's coat, can help you spot any parasites early. Keeping your yard clean and free from standing water can also reduce the mosquito population in your area.

Remember, preventive veterinary medicine is a crucial part of maintaining your senior Goldendoodle's overall health and quality of life. By staying proactive in flea, tick, and heartworm prevention, you are providing your Goldendoodle with the best chance at a happy and healthy seniorhood.

In conclusion, preventive parasite control is a vital aspect of caring for your senior Goldendoodle. By following your veterinarian's recommendations and implementing preventive measures, you can protect your furry friend from the discomfort and potential health risks associated with fleas, ticks, and heartworms. Stay vigilant, stay proactive, and enjoy many more years of joy and companionship with your senior Goldendoodle.

Chapter 10: Preventive Reproductive Health Care for Senior Goldendoodle Dogs

Spaying or Neutering Senior Goldendoodles

As your beloved Goldendoodle enters their senior years, it's important to consider their overall health and well-being. One aspect of preventive veterinary medicine that should be taken into account is whether or not to spay or neuter your senior Goldendoodle. This decision can have a significant impact on their overall health and quality of life.

Spaying or neutering a senior Goldendoodle can help prevent certain health issues that may arise in their later years. For female Goldendoodles, spaying can eliminate the risk of uterine infections and reduce the chances of developing mammary tumors. Neutering male Goldendoodles can help prevent testicular cancer and reduce the risk of prostate problems.

Another important consideration is the prevention of unwanted litters. Even in their senior years, Goldendoodles can still reproduce, and accidental pregnancies can pose risks to their health. By spaying or neutering your senior Goldendoodle, you can eliminate the risk of unplanned pregnancies and potential complications that may arise.

It's essential to discuss the spaying or neutering procedure with your veterinarian, as they can provide personalized recommendations based on your Goldendoodle's individual needs and health history. They will consider factors such as your dog's age, overall health, and any existing medical conditions before making a recommendation.

While the spaying or neutering procedure is generally safe for senior Goldendoodles, there are potential risks involved. It's crucial to have a thorough pre-surgical examination performed by your veterinarian to assess your dog's overall health and ensure they are fit for the procedure. Your veterinarian will also provide guidance on post-operative care to ensure a smooth recovery.

In summary, spaying or neutering your senior Goldendoodle can have several benefits, including the prevention of certain health issues and the elimination of the risk of unplanned pregnancies. However, it's important to consult with your veterinarian before making a decision and to consider your dog's individual circumstances. By taking preventive measures, such as spaying or neutering, you can help ensure a healthier and happier life for your senior Goldendoodle.

Managing Reproductive Health Risks in Senior Goldendoodles

As our beloved Goldendoodles enter their senior years, it is essential to pay close attention to their reproductive health and take preventive measures to ensure their well-being. In this chapter, we will discuss the various reproductive health risks that senior Goldendoodles may face and explore strategies to manage these risks effectively.

One common reproductive health risk in senior Goldendoodles is the development of reproductive tumors, such as ovarian or testicular cancer. These tumors can be life-threatening if not detected and treated early. Therefore, regular veterinary check-ups and screenings are crucial to identify any abnormalities and initiate prompt treatment.

Additionally, senior Goldendoodles may experience hormonal imbalances, such as hypothyroidism or hyperadrenocorticism, which can affect their reproductive health. These conditions can lead to infertility, irregular heat cycles, or other reproductive complications. By monitoring their hormone levels through routine blood tests, veterinarians can identify and manage these imbalances effectively.

Another reproductive health risk that senior Goldendoodles may face is the development of prostate problems in males. Prostate enlargement or infection can cause urinary difficulties and discomfort. Regular prostate examinations and screenings can help identify any abnormalities and prevent potential complications.

Spaying or neutering senior Goldendoodles can also play a significant role in managing reproductive health risks. These procedures eliminate the risk of certain reproductive cancers and can help prevent unwanted behaviors associated with intact animals, such as roaming or aggression.

Furthermore, responsible breeding practices should be considered when it comes to senior Goldendoodles. Breeding dogs at an advanced age can pose health risks for both the mother and the puppies. It is essential to consult with a veterinarian and make informed decisions regarding breeding plans for senior Goldendoodles.

By actively managing reproductive health risks in senior Goldendoodles, we can ensure their overall well-being and longevity. Regular veterinary check-ups, hormone level monitoring, and spaying or neutering can significantly reduce the likelihood of reproductive complications and promote a healthier and happier life for our beloved companions.

In the next chapter, we will discuss preventive emotional and behavioral care for senior Goldendoodles, exploring strategies to address common age-related behavioral changes and promote their mental well-being. Stay tuned for valuable insights on how to support your senior Goldendoodle's emotional and behavioral health.

Regular Reproductive Health Exams for Senior Goldendoodles

As our beloved Goldendoodles age, it becomes increasingly important to prioritize their overall health and well-being. While many aspects of senior care, such as joint and mobility care or cognitive health, are commonly discussed, reproductive health is often overlooked. However, regular reproductive health exams are crucial for maintaining the overall health and happiness of senior Goldendoodles.

Reproductive health exams for senior Goldendoodles involve a comprehensive assessment of their reproductive organs, including the uterus, ovaries, and mammary glands. These exams are essential for early detection and prevention of reproductive diseases, such as uterine infections or mammary tumors.

One of the primary concerns for senior Goldendoodles is the risk of developing pyometra, a potentially life-threatening infection of the uterus. Regular reproductive health exams allow veterinarians to monitor the health of the uterus and identify any signs of infection or abnormalities. Early detection and treatment of pyometra are crucial to ensure the best possible outcome for our furry friends.

Additionally, mammary tumors are relatively common in female dogs as they age. Regular exams enable veterinarians to monitor the mammary glands and identify any lumps or abnormalities. Early detection of mammary tumors significantly increases the chances of successful treatment and recovery.

For male Goldendoodles, regular reproductive health exams can help identify any abnormalities or signs of prostate disease. Prostate issues become more prevalent in aging male dogs and can lead to discomfort, difficulty urinating, or even infertility. Timely intervention and treatment can prevent further complications and improve the quality of life for our senior Goldendoodles.

During reproductive health exams, veterinarians may also discuss and recommend options for spaying or neutering senior Goldendoodles. While this decision is ultimately up to the pet owner, it is crucial to understand the potential benefits and risks associated with these procedures in older dogs.

In conclusion, regular reproductive health exams are an essential component of preventive veterinary medicine for senior Goldendoodles. By prioritizing their reproductive health, we can ensure that our beloved companions lead happy, healthy, and fulfilling lives in their golden years. Remember, early detection and prevention are key to maintaining the overall well-being of our senior Goldendoodles.

Chapter 11: Preventive Emotional and Behavioral Care for Senior Goldendoodle Dogs

Senior Goldendoodle's Emotional Health and Well-being

Senior Goldendoodles, like any other aging dog, require special attention to their emotional health and well-being. As our furry friends grow older, they may experience changes in behavior and temperament that can be attributed to a variety of factors, including physical discomfort, cognitive decline, and emotional distress. In this subchapter, we will delve into the importance of preventive emotional and behavioral care for senior Goldendoodle dogs and provide practical tips on how to ensure their overall well-being.

One of the key aspects of promoting emotional health in senior Goldendoodles is maintaining a stable and nurturing environment. As dogs age, they become more sensitive to changes in their surroundings, so it is crucial to provide them with a consistent routine and a comfortable living space. This can be achieved by establishing a designated area for your senior Goldendoodle, where they can rest, relax, and feel safe.

Additionally, regular exercise and mental stimulation are vital for the emotional well-being of senior Goldendoodles. Engaging them in gentle physical activities, such as short walks or light play sessions, can help alleviate boredom and reduce anxiety. Furthermore, providing them with interactive toys and puzzle games can help keep their minds active and prevent cognitive decline.

Another essential aspect of preventive emotional care for senior Goldendoodles is socialization. While they may not have the same energy levels as when they were younger, it is still important to expose them to different environments, people, and other animals. This can be achieved through short outings to parks or pet-friendly establishments, where they can interact with other dogs and humans, promoting a sense of belonging and reducing feelings of isolation.

Lastly, it is crucial to monitor and address any changes in your senior Goldendoodle's behavior. Dogs, like humans, can experience anxiety, depression, and other emotional issues, and it is important to seek professional help if needed. Consulting with a veterinarian or a professional dog behaviorist can provide valuable insights and guidance on how to address and manage any emotional or behavioral changes.

By prioritizing the emotional well-being of your senior Goldendoodle and implementing preventive measures, you can ensure that they enjoy a fulfilling and contented life in their golden years. Remember, a happy and emotionally healthy dog is a cherished companion and a source of joy for the entire family.

Recognizing and Addressing Behavioral Changes in Senior Goldendoodles

As our beloved Goldendoodles age, it is important for us as pet owners to be aware of the behavioral changes they may experience. Just like humans, senior dogs can undergo certain changes in their behavior that may indicate underlying health issues or cognitive decline. In this subchapter, we will explore the various behavioral changes that senior Goldendoodles may exhibit and discuss ways to address and manage them.

One of the most common behavioral changes seen in aging Goldendoodles is an increase in anxiety or restlessness. This can manifest as excessive pacing, panting, or even destructive behavior. It is important to identify the underlying cause of this anxiety and address it accordingly. It may be due to pain, discomfort, or even cognitive decline. Consulting with a veterinarian can help determine the root cause and provide appropriate treatment options.

Another behavior change to watch out for is aggression or irritability. Senior Goldendoodles may become more reactive towards other animals or even family members. This could be a sign of pain, territorial behavior, or cognitive dysfunction. It is crucial to seek professional help to assess the situation and implement behavior modification techniques to ensure the safety of both your pet and those around them.

Additionally, senior Goldendoodles may experience changes in their sleep patterns. They may have difficulty falling asleep or staying asleep, leading to daytime drowsiness or restlessness. This could be due to pain, discomfort, or hormonal imbalances. Creating a comfortable sleep environment, providing regular exercise, and ensuring a consistent routine can help regulate their sleep patterns.

Cognitive decline is also a common issue in senior dogs, including Goldendoodles. They may show signs of confusion, disorientation, or forgetfulness. Engaging in mental stimulation activities, such as puzzle toys or training exercises, can help keep their minds active and slow down cognitive decline.

Lastly, it is important to address any sudden changes in appetite or bathroom habits. Senior Goldendoodles may experience reduced appetite or increased thirst, which could be indicative of an underlying health issue. Frequent urination or accidents in the house may also be signs of urinary tract problems or incontinence.

In conclusion, recognizing and addressing behavioral changes in senior Goldendoodles is crucial for their overall well-being. By being vigilant and proactive, we can ensure that our furry friends receive the appropriate care and support during their golden years. Consulting with a veterinarian, implementing behavior modification techniques, and providing a stimulating environment are all essential steps in maintaining the emotional and behavioral health of our senior Goldendoodles.

Enrichment and Mental Health Support for Senior Goldendoodles

As our beloved Goldendoodles age, it is crucial to prioritize their overall well-being, including their mental health. Just like humans, senior dogs can experience cognitive decline and behavioral changes. However, with the right preventive measures and support, we can help ensure that our furry friends maintain a fulfilling and happy life.

Enrichment activities play a vital role in promoting mental stimulation for senior Goldendoodles. These activities can include puzzle toys, interactive games, and scent work. Engaging their minds through these activities not only provides mental exercise but also helps prevent boredom and destructive behaviors. Additionally, regular walks in different environments and exposure to new sights and sounds can nourish their senses and keep them mentally sharp.

Another essential aspect of mental health support for senior Goldendoodles is maintaining a consistent routine. Dogs thrive on predictability, and a stable daily schedule can provide them with a sense of security and reduce anxiety. Ensuring that they have regular exercise, meals, and social interactions can greatly contribute to their overall well-being.

In some cases, senior Goldendoodles may experience age-related cognitive decline, also known as canine cognitive dysfunction (CCD). This condition can cause memory loss, disorientation, and changes in behavior. To address CCD, there are various preventive measures that can be taken, such as providing a balanced diet rich in antioxidants and omega-3 fatty acids, which have been shown to support brain health. Additionally, mental stimulation, such as training exercises and interactive toys, can help slow down the progression of cognitive decline.

Senior Goldendoodle owners should also be mindful of the emotional well-being of their furry companions. As dogs age, they may become more sensitive to changes in their environment and may require additional support and reassurance. Providing a calm and comforting space, regular social interactions, and maintaining a strong bond with your senior Goldendoodle can go a long way in promoting their emotional health.

In conclusion, enrichment and mental health support are crucial aspects of preventive veterinary medicine for senior Goldendoodles. By incorporating mental stimulation activities, maintaining a consistent routine, addressing age-related cognitive decline, and prioritizing emotional well-being, we can help our furry friends live a fulfilling and happy life in their golden years.

Chapter 12: Conclusion

Recap of Preventive Veterinary Medicine for Senior Goldendoodle Dogs

As your beloved Goldendoodle dog enters their senior years, it becomes even more crucial to prioritize their preventive veterinary care. By taking proactive steps to maintain their health, you can ensure that your furry friend enjoys a happy and comfortable life. In this subchapter, we will recap the key aspects of preventive veterinary medicine for senior Goldendoodle dogs.

Preventive dental care is essential for your senior Goldendoodle's overall health and well-being. Regular teeth brushing, professional cleanings, and dental examinations can prevent tooth decay, gum disease, and other oral health problems that can impact their overall health.

Proper nutrition and diet play a vital role in maintaining your senior Goldendoodle's health. Consult with your veterinarian to develop a balanced and age-appropriate diet that meets their nutritional needs. Adequate hydration, portion control, and the right mix of nutrients are all crucial factors to consider.

Joint and mobility care is particularly important for senior Goldendoodles, as they may be prone to arthritis and other joint issues. Regular exercise, joint supplements, and appropriate pain management can help keep their joints healthy and alleviate discomfort.

Regular eye and vision care is necessary to detect and address any age-related eye conditions early on. Your veterinarian can perform routine eye exams and recommend treatments or interventions to maintain their visual health.

Maintaining a healthy skin and coat is not only aesthetically pleasing but also crucial for your senior Goldendoodle's overall well-being. Regular grooming, including brushing, bathing, and nail trimming, can prevent skin irritations, infections, and other dermatological issues.

Heart and cardiovascular care are vital for senior Goldendoodles, as they may be more prone to heart disease and other cardiovascular conditions. Regular check-ups, heartworm prevention medication, and a heart-healthy diet can help promote a strong and healthy heart.

Cognitive and brain health care is essential in ensuring your senior Goldendoodle's mental sharpness and overall cognitive function. Engage them in stimulating activities, provide mental enrichment toys, and discuss with your veterinarian about potential supplements or treatments to support their cognitive health.

Parasite control is a crucial aspect of preventive veterinary medicine for senior Goldendoodles. Regularly administer flea and tick preventives, keep up with vaccinations, and conduct routine fecal tests to detect and treat any intestinal parasites.

Reproductive health care may not be applicable for senior Goldendoodles that have been spayed or neutered. However, if your dog is intact, consult with your veterinarian to discuss the best reproductive health care options to prevent unwanted pregnancies or reproductive diseases.

Finally, emotional and behavioral care is vital for senior Goldendoodles' overall well-being. Ensure they receive plenty of exercise, mental stimulation, and love to prevent anxiety, depression, and other behavioral issues.

By prioritizing these aspects of preventive veterinary medicine, you can provide your senior Goldendoodle with the best possible care and help them enjoy a long, healthy, and happy life by your side. Remember to consult with your veterinarian for personalized advice and recommendations tailored specifically to your dog's needs.

The Importance of Regular Vet Visits and Preventive Care

Regular veterinary visits and preventive care are essential for maintaining the health and well-being of your senior Goldendoodle dog. As your furry companion ages, it becomes even more crucial to prioritize preventive veterinary medicine to ensure a long, happy, and healthy life.

Preventive veterinary medicine encompasses a wide range of areas, including dental care, nutrition and diet, joint and mobility care, eye and vision care, skin and coat care, heart and cardiovascular care, cognitive and brain health care, parasite control, reproductive health care, and emotional and behavioral care. Each of these aspects plays a significant role in maintaining your senior Goldendoodle's overall health and quality of life.

Regular vet visits are the foundation of preventive care. These visits allow your veterinarian to assess your dog's overall health, identify any potential issues, and provide the necessary treatments or interventions. During these visits, your vet will perform a thorough physical examination, discuss any concerns or changes you've noticed, and update your dog's vaccinations and preventatives.

Dental care is particularly crucial for senior Goldendoodle dogs. Periodontal disease is a common issue in older dogs and can lead to pain, tooth loss, and even systemic health problems. Regular dental cleanings and examinations can help prevent or address dental issues, ensuring your dog's mouth stays healthy.

Proper nutrition and diet are also essential for senior Goldendoodle dogs. As your dog ages, their dietary needs may change, and they may require specific nutrients or supplements to support their overall health. Your veterinarian can guide you in selecting the right diet and feeding regimen for your senior Goldendoodle.

Joint and mobility care is another critical aspect of preventive veterinary medicine for senior Goldendoodle dogs. Regular exercise, weight management, and joint supplements can help maintain your dog's mobility and prevent or manage conditions like arthritis.

Regular eye and vision care, skin and coat care, heart and cardiovascular care, cognitive and brain health care, parasite control, reproductive health care, and emotional and behavioral care are all important components of preventive veterinary medicine for senior Goldendoodle dogs. Your veterinarian can provide guidance on specific preventive measures, such as regular eye examinations, skin and coat health, heartworm prevention, cognitive stimulation, and behavior management.

By prioritizing regular vet visits and preventive care, you can help ensure that your senior Goldendoodle dog enjoys a happy, healthy, and fulfilling life. Your veterinarian is a valuable partner in your dog's overall healthcare journey, providing expert guidance and support to address any concerns and keep your dog's health at its best.

Tips for Maintaining Your Senior Goldendoodle's Overall Health and Well-being

As your beloved Senior Goldendoodle enters the golden years of their life, it's crucial to prioritize their health and well-being. By implementing preventive veterinary medicine strategies, you can ensure that your furry friend enjoys a happy and healthy life for years to come. This subchapter will provide you with valuable tips and insights on various aspects of preventive care tailored specifically for Senior Goldendoodles.

1. Preventive Veterinary Medicine for a Senior Goldendoodle Dog:

Regular visits to a trusted veterinarian are essential for maintaining your dog's overall health. Schedule routine check-ups, vaccinations, and screenings to catch any potential health issues early on.

2. Preventive Dental Care for Senior Goldendoodle Dogs:

Maintaining good oral hygiene is crucial to prevent dental diseases in senior Goldendoodles. Brush their teeth regularly, provide dental treats, and consider professional cleanings when necessary.

3. Preventive Nutrition and Diet for Senior Goldendoodle Dogs:

A well-balanced diet is key to promoting your dog's overall health. Consult with your veterinarian to create a diet plan that meets their specific nutritional needs as they age.

4. Preventive Joint and Mobility Care for Senior Goldendoodle Dogs:

Arthritis and joint problems are common in aging dogs. Regular exercise, joint supplements, and providing a comfortable and supportive sleeping area can help alleviate these issues.

5. Preventive Eye and Vision Care for Senior Goldendoodle Dogs:

Regular eye examinations and cleaning can help identify any eye-related health issues. Ensure their eyes are clear and free from any discharge or redness.

6. Preventive Skin and Coat Care for Senior Goldendoodle Dogs:

Proper grooming, regular bathing, and checking for any skin abnormalities can help prevent skin infections and keep their coat healthy and shiny.

7. Preventive Heart and Cardiovascular Care for Senior Goldendoodle Dogs:

Maintaining a healthy weight and providing regular exercise can help prevent heart diseases. Regular check-ups can also help monitor their heart health.

8. Preventive Cognitive and Brain Health Care for Senior Goldendoodle Dogs:

Engage your senior Goldendoodle in mental stimulation activities to keep their brain sharp. Puzzle toys, obedience training, and interactive playtime can help prevent cognitive decline.

9. Preventive Parasite Control for Senior Goldendoodle Dogs:

Regularly administer flea, tick, and heartworm prevention treatments as recommended by your veterinarian to keep your dog protected from parasites.

10. Preventive Reproductive Health Care for Senior Goldendoodle Dogs:

Spaying or neutering your senior Goldendoodle can help prevent certain health issues and reduce the risk of certain cancers.

11. Preventive Emotional and Behavioral Care for Senior Goldendoodle Dogs:

Ensure your dog receives plenty of love, attention, and mental stimulation to maintain their emotional well-being. Consider behavioral training or therapy if needed.

By following these valuable tips for maintaining your Senior Goldendoodle's overall health and well-being, you can provide them with a happy and comfortable life in their senior years. Remember, preventive care is the key to a long and fulfilling life for your furry friend.

9 798822 376882